# MAGIC MIRROR

## THE SACRED QUIMBANDA ORACLE OF EXU

***CARLOS ANTONIO DE BOURBON-GALDIANO-MONTENEGRO***

**AMERICAN CANDOMBLE CHURCH PUBLICATIONS, LOS ANGELES, CALIFORNIA**

# MAGIC MIRROR

## THE SACRED QUIMBANDA ORACLE OF EXU



**AMERICAN CANDOMBLE CHURCH PUBLICATIONS**

**P.O. BOX 881377**

**LOS ANGELES, CALIFORNIA 90009**

**LEGAL DISCLAIMER**

No part of this book may be reproduced in any manner without written permission from the publisher or the author of this book. This book contains formulas that were used in the historical AFRO-BRAZILIAN religious practices of Quimbanda, Candomble, Macumba and Umbanda. The author and the publisher do not encourage any of the practices in this book nor do we assume any liabilities for presenting those formulas or any information in this book. The formulas and information is presented for curious only. Neither the author, *Carlos Antonio De Bourbon-Galdiano-Montenegro* nor the publisher, *American Candomble Church* assumes any responsibilities for the outcome of any of the spells, rituals or initiations in this book. We make no claims to any supernatural powers of these traditional initiation rituals. All inquiries or comments may be directed to the publisher. You must be at least 18 years of age or older to purchase this book or to purchase any of the supplies listed herein.

**TABLE OF CONTENTS**

# INTRODUCTION

The following partial manuscript was taken from the original magical *Grimoire* of my late *Great Uncle, Chico Ita- Montenegro* which is now in my possession. It is a translation from its original Portuguese version. Although the following manuscript is only a partial selection of the original manuscript from this very powerful book of shadows estimated to have been written by my uncle between the years of 1910 and 1950, the magical formula on how to construct the ***Montenegro Quimbanda Magic Mirror*** is an invaluable artifact of the history of the occult, the supernatural and Latin American Spiritualism. If time permits and with the permission of the *Quimbanda Trinity* and of course the Spirit of *Chico Ita-Montenegro*, I may sometime in the future present the entire Grimoire to the occult world as a tribute and historical account of one man's legacy in the world of the Afro-Brazilian religious tradition known as *Quimbanda* and Latin American Sorcery. A sacred world shrouded in mystery, rich folklore and forgotten ancient magical mysteries to invoke and to awaken the power of the Universe. The following magical formula of how to prepare the *Montenegro Quimbanda Magic Mirror* and how to give it life must be followed exactly how it was presented in the original Grimoire of *Chico Ita-Montenegro*. If it is not followed exactly and correctly, the results can be detrimental to your physical, emotional and spiritual well-being. My name is *Carlos Antonio De Bourbon-Galdiano- Montenegro* and I present to you in the following occult manuscript of my family, the cosmic keys to unlock the sacred door to the mysterious world and realm of the invisibles. This wonderful world of forbidden knowledge, I know too well.

SARAVA

***CARLOS ANTONIO DE BOURBON-GALDIANO-MONTENEGRO***

May 15, 2011

## THE HISTORY OF THE MONTENEGRO MAGIC MIRROR

In the 1920's the *Montenegro Family* immigrated to the United States. When they immigrated they also brought with them a very rich Afro-Brazilian religious tradition known as *Quimbanda*. The *Montenegro Family* were the first individuals to bring this very powerful form of spirituality to the United States. Our family's religious tradition in Afro- Brazilian *Quimbanda* and the Orixa religious tradition known as *Candomblé De Congo* will be celebrating our 150th Year Anniversary on May 1, 2013. I was initiated into the mysteries of *Afro-Brazilian Quimbanda* by my *Great Uncle, Chico Ita-Montenegro*. *Uncle Chico* was a *Quimbandeiro Priest* who had very extraordinary supernatural powers. There are so many stories about this strange man who disappeared so many years ago. At any rate, let's begin his incredible story. *Uncle Chico* occasionally traveled to Los Angeles to visit my *Great Grand Mother, Maria Miranda De Bourbon- Montenegro*. Both of my Great Grand-Parents had both grown up together in the old country (Brazil) with *Uncle Chico*. *Chico* was also an *Orixa Priest* of the Afro-Brazilian religious tradition known *Candomblé De Congo*. *Uncle Chico* never married and when I met him he was in late seventies. *Chico* was from the famous *Afro-Brazilian Candomblé* center of *Bahia*. *Bahia* is one of the 26 States of Brazil, and is located in the Northeastern part of the country on the Atlantic coast. Bahia's capital is the *City of Salvador*, or more properly, *São Salvador da Bahia de Todos os Santos*, and is located at the junction of the Atlantic Ocean and the *Bay of All Saints*, first seen by European sailors in 1501. The name "*bahia*" is an archaic spelling of the Portuguese word *baía*, meaning "*bay*". In one legend it was rumored that early in *Chico's* youth, he and two of his friends had made a pact with the Angel Lucifer. Sometime after the ceremony the two friends mysteriously disappeared. The story goes that when he was about 17 years old, he and his two friends went into the old local cemetery where they had buried many of the slaves in the old days. They went there to communicate with the spirits and to also collect the ritual items (bones and graveyard dirt) necessary to construct an nganga (a traditional Congo spirit pot). When the time of 12 midnight came, they began to invoke the spirits to manifest so that they could capture one, but the spirit that manifested wasn't the one that they had summoned. The spirit manifested in the form of a brilliant illuminating glowing light and then took the form of an old black man. Sometime later it would be revealed that the spirit that manifested was *Exu Marabo. Exu Marabo* is sometimes identified with the devil and is the trickster spirit who lives at the crossroads. *Exu Marabo* is also the messenger for the powerful *Quimbanda Spirit, Exu Rei*. The particular type of the nganga that *Uncle Chico* was collecting the items in the cemetery was for an unbaptized spirit known as "*nganga judeu*" (unbaptized spirit nganga). The spirit of the "*Nganga Judeu*" is one of the most powerful of the *Congo nkisi* spirits that a *Quimbandeiro* can possess. It is also one of the most evil and feared. The spirit said to the three boys, "I know why you have come", "I can offer you more than these old spirits here". The spirit then said, "I can offer you things beyond your wildest dreams". *Chico* who was the youngest of the three boys was a little cautious at first, but listened to the spirit talk. The oldest boy asked the spirit what they needed to do and the spirit said, "you must sell me your souls". The two older boys agreed because of their greed, but *Chico* said, "I'll only sell you ¾ of my soul". The spirit agreed and instructed them what to do. Together they dug the graves. *Chico* unearthed the bones of an old man that the spirit had instructed him to take. *Chico* then placed them into a burlap sack and carried away the bones of the spirit into the night. *Chico* who lived with his family just outside of town worked on the sugar cane fields. It took many days and nights to ritually prepare the "*nganga judeu*" but after it was complete he began practicing the sacred magical art of Quimbanda and Latin American necromancy and working with it. There are many classic stories about *Uncle Chico* that I remember my family telling me as a child. The first story involved a traveling magic show and carnival that came to town each year. One year, the magic show had an amateur's day and *Chico* decided to go and try and win the cash prize. *Chico* secretly took his burlap spirit sack along with him. When it was his turn to pull a rabbit out of the hat or pull out flowers from his sleeve, *Chico* did something completely different. *Chico* placed his burlap spirit sack next to him and he began to invoke and summon the spirit. The majority of the people who were in attendance at the magic show were unaware of what he was doing, but when he finished, he raised his hands to the sky and it started to rain only in the area were the audience stood. The crowd became alarmed because this wasn't circus magic, it was black magic. The people started to throw stones at *Chico*. The people called him the devil and then chased him all the way to the edge of the city. This event was extremely significant in the life of *Chico* because it forced him to move away from his family to live in a remote area by himself. By isolating himself from the town's people, *Chico* was able to study and practice his Latin American sorcery without any intervention or interference from the outside world. In another story, it was said that a well-known *Pai-de-Santo* had died in a nearby city. A *Pai-de-Santo* is an initiated Orixa Priest of the African religious tradition known as *Candomblé*. The nearby city was exactly 6 hours from where *Chico* lived. *Chico's* brother *Domingo* came by his home to see if he wanted to go with a small group of individuals from town to pay their respects. *Chico* said no, because some years before he and the *Pai-de-Santo* had an argument and had not spoken to each other in quite some time. *Chico's* brother and the small group of individuals got in the car to leave early in the morning in order for them to arrive at the "wake" because it was a long six hour ride on a dirt road. When the group arrived at the home of the deceased *Pai-de-Santo*, *Chico* was already sitting in the corner. *Chico* according to the eye witnesses had arrived there three hours before them. How could this have happened since *Chico* did not drive or own a vehicle? In yet another story, *Chico* liked to perform supernatural magic tricks for his close friends and family. My Grandfather told me that one day *Chico* came over his house to eat dinner. After dinner, my Great Aunts and Uncles who were teenagers at the time always begged *Chico* to perform some magic for them. *Chico* agreed and went into one of the side parlor rooms. While in private, he began to pray to his spirit. *Chico* never traveled without his spirit sack and he would never let anyone see the inside contents. It is surprisingly how he got his spirit back and forth from

America and back to Brazil undetected by the United States Customs authorities. The only thing that anyone really knew for sure is that there was something spiritually alive inside his mysterious spiritual burlap sack. The doors were closed, but my Aunt remembers sneaking up to the door to secretly listen. She said that she remembers hearing him speak to someone, but no one else was permitted to enter into the room with him. *Chico* came out of the parlor room into the living room which was filled with kids and adults and closed his eyes, raised his hands and began to swing his arms in the air. All of a sudden, my Grandmothers broom came gliding out of the kitchen floating in the mid-air and it began to dance and bounce around for a few minutes and then would fall to the ground. Events like things were commonplace in the *Montenegro Family* home whenever *Uncle Chico* came into town and stayed for dinner.

In another story, it was said that because *Chico* had only sold only ¾ of his soul to the devil, the devil was constantly hounding and bothering him for the other ¼ of his soul. It was said that at night, the devil would send spiritual messengers in the form of screaming black cats to scratch on the outside windows of the room where *Uncle Chico* slept. These events were all witnessed by credible individuals, many of whom are still alive today to confirm the actual happenings. This story was quite frightening to me as a child. Every time that I heard the stories about *Chico*, I became afraid and my Grandmother seeing the scared expression on my face would begin to laugh. One night on one of *Chico's* visits to my Great Grand Mother's home, I had to sleep in the same room with him. Sometime after 12 midnight,

I heard an animal scratching at the outside bedroom window and making a strange cry. I pulled the blankets over my head and prayed that whatever was outside would hopefully go away. I'm not sure if it was the devil coming to collect the ¼ remaining part of *Chico's* soul, but it sure scared the hell out of me. In another story, I remember *Chico* taking me into my Grandmother's *Quimbanda* and *Candomble* ritual altar room that was located outside her residence. The altar room housed all of the spiritual mysteries and sacred ingredients necessary to do magic rituals. I remember that he and my Grandmother were trying to find out what their enemies were doing. *Chico* would always bring out his sacred divination magic mirror to discover what was going on. The mirror, which was a sacred oracle, was used to look into the doings and whereabouts of their enemies. The magic mirror was made inside of a large clay bowl. The bowl was filled with water and after a very lengthy magic ritual he would then began to look into the water in the bowl and start to reveal things that the spirits allowed him to see. This *Quimbanda* Magic Mirror was an invaluable magical divination tool to determine events and answers to present situation and also to upcoming spiritual events. The Quimbanda Magic Mirror was only used by Chico in times of great necessity when the answers of questions about our enemies needed to be answered quickly and precisely.

The last story is about the disappearance of *Uncle Chico*. In the early 1980's, *Chico* returned back to live in Brazil and was officially placed on the missing person's list in Brazil. To this day, nothing is known about his whereabouts or the exact time of his disappearance. It is quite obvious that by now that he must be dead. When he and his spirit disappeared it was rumored that the devil had finally come to collect his payment. Many years later, *Chico's* very secret *Quimbanda Grimoire* of magical spells, rituals and spiritual incantations somehow appeared in the personal items of my Great Grandmother when she died. I am now in possession of this very powerful *Grimoire* of Latin American sorcery and original rituals of the *Quimbanda* religious tradition.

## HOW TO PREPARE THE MONTENEGRO MAGIC MIRROR

The *Quimbanda Magic Mirror* is a scrying mirror that can be used to see the movements of your enemies and to spy on them. The word scrying comes from the old English word "descry", meaning "to see" or "to observe." Scrying is a form of clairvoyance that usually uses mirrors, crystals, a bowl of water, or other scrying devices. The *Quimbanda Magic Mirror* is a great addition to your spiritual tools as it can foretell things both good and bad to come. By using this magic mirror you will be able to be one step ahead of your occult enemies and thus it will allow you to prepare and to take action to stop them from continuing to harm you. Once you have prepared your *Quimbanda Magic Mirror* you can keep it on your spiritual altar until ready to use. The following formula of how to prepare a *Quimbanda Magic Mirror* was given to me by my late *Great Uncle, Chico Ita-Montenegro*, a very powerful Brazilian Quimbandeiro whos powers were well documented. Because my family was heavily involved in European sorcery before they arrived in Brazil in the 1800's, this formula was given to my Uncle *Chico Ita-Montenegro* by the Congo spirits when he was initiated into the *Afro-Brazilian Quimbanda* mysteries. The *Quimbanda Magic Mirror* is a mixture of European and Afro-Brazilian magical traditions. After he made the first *Quimbanda Magic Mirror* it was then adopted by other Quimbanda temples. Although the formula to prepare one was a well-guarded secret by my family for many years, we would like to share it with you in this book so you will have a powerful tool to defend yourself against your occult enemies. The process to prepare the *Quimbanda Magic Mirror* is quite complicated, but you must prepare it exactly as I have written here if you want to get real magical results. I also want to say that once you have made and prepared your *Quimbanda Magic Mirror,* never allow anyone else to touch it or even look into it. The *Quimbanda Magic Mirror* must be covered at all times with a black cloth. The power of the *Quimbanda Magic Mirror* is so strong that it opens up a doorway into the mystical world of the realm of the spirits and demons. The *Quimbanda Magic Mirror* can also be used to change the destiny of an individual by seeing it before it happens. The *Quimbanda Magic Mirror* is perhaps one of the strongest forms of authentic magical divining tools to deliver a sacred oracle with almost 100% accuracy. The following instructions and magical ritual formula were taken directly out of the original personal *Quimbanda Grimoire* of my *Uncle Chico Ita-Montenegro* after he departed and left this world to begin his journey on the other side. The original ritual formula instructions were in Portuguese and it has been translated into English for the purpose of this manuscript. Some of the herbs used in this book have been changed and substituted for herbs found in Caribbean magical practices because they are difficult to find. Authentic Brazilian herbs used in the practical application of magical rituals are difficult to find in the United States. Either way, I have used the formula presented here in this book using the magical herbal substitutes and had really good results. I would also like to note that the *Quimbanda Magic Mirror* is not a regular divination tool used by traditional *Afro-Brazilian Quimbanda Priests*. The formula to prepare the *Quimbanda Magic Mirror* was presented to my Great Uncle, Chico Ita-Montenegro by the powerful Spirit, Exu Marabo.

## A SPIRITUAL WARNING

*DO NOT ATTEMPT TO PREPARE THE QUIMBANDA MAGIC MIRROR IF YOU ARE NOT READY TO SEE AND DEAL WITH THE FUTURE. SOMETIMES NOT KNOWING IS BETTER. THE CHOICE IS UP TO YOU. REMEMBER THE QUIMBANDA MAGIC MIRROR IS A PORTAL AND A DOORWAY TO THE MYSTICAL SUPERNATURAL WORLD OF THE BEYOND. THE QUIMBANDA MAGIC MIRROR WILL OPEN THE DOORS TO CONNECT THE WORLD OF THE LIVING AND THE DEAD. USE IT WISELY AND DO NOT ABUSE ITS SACRED POWERS. MAKE SURE AFTER USING THE QUIMBANDA MAGIC MIRROR THAT YOU DO THE RITUAL TO CLOSE ITS DOORS OR IT CAN ACT LIKE A DOORWAY FOR EVIL SPIRITS AND DEMONS TO PASS THROUGH AND CROSS OVER INTO OUR WORLD AND REMAIN HERE CAUSING GREAT SUFFERING AND MISERY.*

***USE THE QUIMBANDA MAGIC MIRROR AT YOUR OWN RISK.***

*SARAVA*

## HOW TO PREPARE THE QUIMBANDA MAGIC MIRROR

<u>*Items Needed*</u>

*One large round clay bowl, One mirror that has been cut to fit perfectly to the entire bottom of the clay bowl, Human bone from 7 Men, Human bone from 7 Females, Crushed Quartz Crystals, Rust Powder, Copper Filings, Iron Filings, Dirt from 7 Tombs of men, Dirt from 7 Tombs of women, Dirt from 7 Crossroads, Dirt from 7 Catholic Churches, Dirt from the Gates of 7 Cemeteries, Crushed Powdered Bones from a Raven, Liquid Mercury, Spirit Omiero consisting of 21 herbs sacred to the Spirit Exu, Black Rooster, Black paint, Red paint, Cement, Cowrie shells (21),Black Pillar Candle (ritually fixed)*

## *Ritual Step - 1*

*THE RITUAL OF PREPARING THE QUIMBANDA MAGIC MIRROR STARTS ON A FULL MOON AT 12 MIDNIGHT. THE ENTIRE RITUAL PREPARATION OF THE QUIMBANDA MAGIC MIRROR MUST BE FINISHED AND COMPLETED BEFORE THE LIGHT OF DAY AND BEFORE THE SUN AWAKENS THE EARTH. THIS PARTICULAR SACRED TIME IS CALLED TWILIGHT. TWILIGHT IS THE TIME WHEN THE SUN IS BELOW THE HORIZON LINE. IF THE RITUAL PREPARATION IS NOT FINISHED BEFORE THE LIGHT OF DAY, THE POWER OF THE QUIMBANDA MAGIC MIRROR WILL NOT WORK. THE ENTIRE RITUAL SHOULD BE DONE OUTSIDE SO THAT THE RAYS OF THE FULL MOON WILL EMPOWER THE QUIMBANDA MAGIC MIRROR AND GIVE ENTRANCE INTO THE REALM OF THE SPIRITS.*

- ***START AND BEGIN THIS RITUAL AT 12 MIDNIGHT ON A FULL MOON*** -

## Ritual Step - 2

Holding a black pillar candle in your hands, light it and pass over the front of your body in the form of the Catholic sign of the cross and afterwards hold it up high above your head and recite the following prayer:

*Ago Exu - Sarava, Ago Exu - Sarava, Ago Exu - Sarava,*

*It was you O Mighty Nzambi who created the Heavens and the Earth.*

*It was you O Mighty Nzambi who created man.*

*It was you O Mighty Nzambi who came to Earth to deliver us from our enemies.*

*It is you O Mighty Nzambi, who gives me victory over my enemies.*

*SARAVA*

## Ritual Step - 3

*Set the bowl down in the ritual area.*

*Place the lighted black candle in a candle holder and place it next to the ritual area where you will begin to prepare the Quimbanda Magic Mirror.*

## Ritual Step - 4

*Prepare a liquid herbal mixture sacred to the Quimbanda Spirit, Exu. The spirit liquid consists of 21 herbs sacred to the Spirit, Exu. This liquid is known by initiates of the Quimbanda religious tradition as "Amaci".*

## Ritual Step - 5

*Combine all of the following ingredients into a large stone mortar and pestle: Human bone from 7 Men, Human bone from 7 Females, Crushed Quartz Crystals, Rust Powder from old Metal Iron Tools, Copper Filings, Iron Filings, Dirt from 7 Tombs of Men, Dirt from 7 Tombs of Women, Dirt from 7 Crossroads, Dirt from the entrance of 7 Catholic Churches, Dirt from the Gates of 7 Cemeteries, Crushed Powdered Bones from a Raven.*

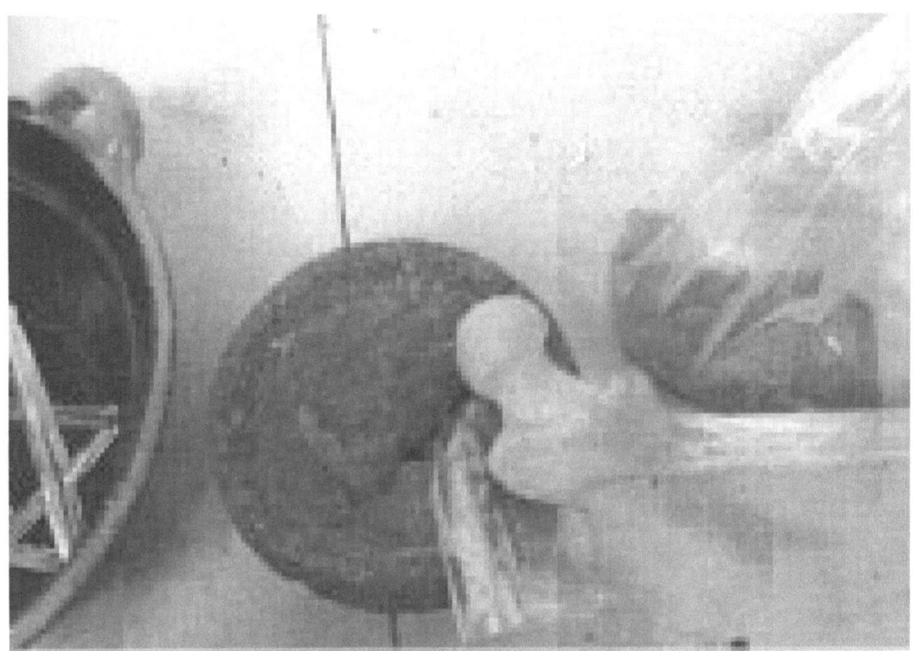

## Ritual Step - 6

*Using the stone mortar and pestle, begin to crush all of the items into a very fine powder.*

## Ritual Step - 7

*Wash the mirror and the clay bowl using the liquid spirit "Amaci" and allow it to dry off thoroughly.*

## Ritual Step - 8

*Open up all of the backs of the 21 Cowrie Shells using a sharp tool to pry them open.*

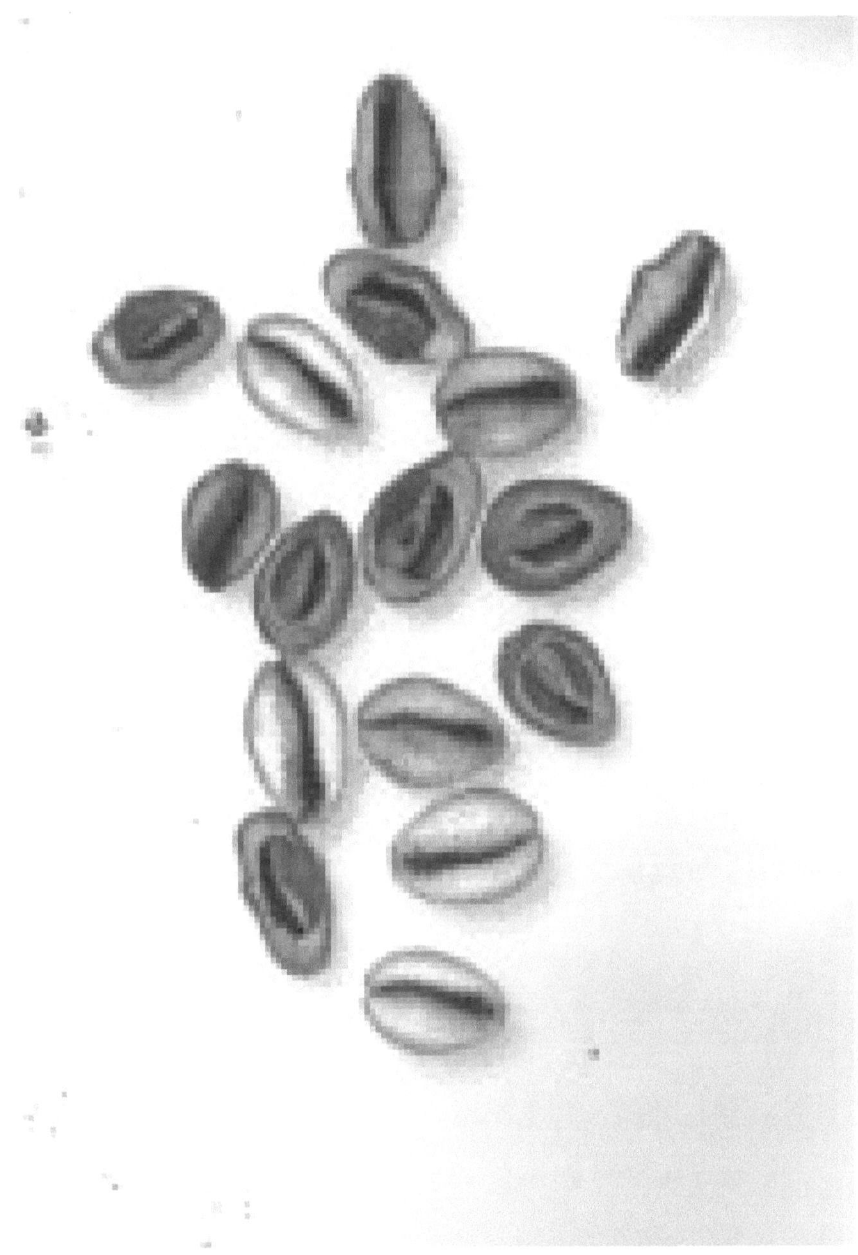

## Ritual Step - 9

*After the clay bowl has completely dried then paint the entire bottom on the inside of the clay bowl using black paint.*

*After the black paint has dried then using the red paint, carefully paint the magical spirit signature in the inside center of the clay bowl.*

*The spirit signature is a powerful key to open up the doorway to the world of the Quimbanda spirits.*

## Ritual Step - 10

*After the paint has dried on the inside of the clay bowl do the following:*

*Pour about ¼ pound of liquid mercury into the clay bowl.*

*Liquid mercury keeps the spirits moving around in the Quimbanda Magic Mirror and allows for a very clear vision and message from the realm of the spirits*

*Sprinkle a generous amount of the crushed powder into the bowl to completely cover the painted area and the magical spirit signature.*

*The amount should come up to about a ¼ inch thick layer in the bowl.*

## Ritual Step - 11

*Sprinkle a small amount of the spirit "Amaci" over all of the ingredients in the clay bowl.*

## Ritual Step - 12

*Using some of the crushed mixture from the mortar and pestle, stuff and insert the powder directly into the backs of the 21 cowrie shells and then seal with the wax from the black candle.*

*Allow them to completely dry.*

## Ritual Step - 13

*Place the mirror facing up directly on top of the crushed ingredients into the center of the clay dish.*

## Ritual Step - 14

*Make a cement mixture and thick paste using fast dry cement and adding a small amount of the crushed ingredients from the mortar and pestle.* The finished magic mirror without cowrie shells.

## Ritual Step - 15

*Place the cement mixture carefully around the outer edges of the mirror in the clay dish to seal it into the bowl firmly so it won't fall out.*

*A picture of the magic mirror setting in front of the Quimbanda spirit nganga of Exu Meia Noite.*

## Ritual Step - 16

*Place the prepared cowrie shells along the outer edges of the clay dish around the mirror and push them into the wet cement mixture.*

*The mouths of the cowrie shells should be facing outwards and facing up.*

## Ritual Step - 17

*Place the completed Quimbanda Magic Mirror next to the black candle and allow it to dry.*

## Ritual Step - 18

*Prepare a Quimbanda ritual magic pillar candle to use when you are invoking the spirits that speak through the Quimbanda Magic Mirror.*

*To prepare the Quimbanda ritual candle do the following:*

*Melt black bees wax and then add the remaining crushed ingredients from the mortar and pestle to it.*

*Pour the hot liquid black bee's wax into a pillar candle mold.*

## Ritual Step - 19

*After the Quimbanda ritual magic pillar candle has completely dried and has been removed from the mold, place it into the Quimbanda Magic Mirror clay bowl.*

## Ritual Step - 20

*Wrap the Quimbanda Magic Mirror, a blessed metal crucifix and the Quimbanda ritual candle in a black cotton cloth.*

*Take the Quimbanda Magic Mirror and its ritual contents to a cemetery and burry in a hole along with 21 pennies at the foot or base of a tombstone shaped in the form of a cross.*

*Leave the lighted black candle that you first began the ritual with burning at the base of the tombstone.*

*Pour Cachaça (Brazilian Sugar Cane liquor) in and around the area of the tombstone.*

*Light a cigar and blow the smoke directly on the tombstone.*

*Before leaving the cemetery, knock three times on the tombstone.*

*After this ritual has been completed leave the cemetery.*

## Ritual Step - 21

*Leave the Quimbanda Magic Mirror and the ritual items buried in the cemetery for 21 days.*

**On the evening of the 21st day go to the cemetery at 12 midnight and do the following ritual:**

*Before unearthing the Quimbanda Magic Mirror and its ritual contents, do the following;*

*Pour Cachaça (Brazilian Sugar Cane liquor) in and around the area of the tombstone.*

*Light a cigar and blow the smoke directly on the tombstone.*

*Place a white candle into the ground at the foot of the tombstone and light it.*

*Knock three times on the tombstone.*

**After knocking three times on the tombstone say the following:**

*Ago - Exu Maioral - Sarava*
*Ago - Exu Rei - Sarava*
*Ago - Maria Padilla Reina - Sarava*
*Ago - Exu Rei Kalunga - Sarava*
*Ago - Pomba Gira Reina Kalunga - Sarava*
*Ago - Exu Porteira - Sarava*
*Ago - Exu Sete Tumbas - Sarava*
*Ago - Exu Sete Catacumbas - Sarava*
*Ago - Exu Da Brasa - Sarava*

*Ago - Exu Caveira - Sarava*
*Ago - Exu Kalunga - Sarava*
*Ago - Exu Corcunda - Sarava*
*Ago - Exu Sete Covas - Sarava*
*Ago - Exu Capa Preta - Sarava*

**Completely unearth the Quimbanda Magic Mirror with the blessed metal crucifix and the ritual black candle and hold it up over your head with both hands and towards the direction of the moon and say the following:**

*Behold the Sacred Light of Truth of the world of the living and the dead.*

*Behold the Sacred Light of Truth of the living word.*

*Behold the Sacred Light which illuminates the doorway of man and spirit.*

*Behold the Sacred Light which has given life and has caused this ritual into being.*

*Behold the Sacred Light of Truth which gives man the invisible sight.*

*Sarava*

## Ritual Step - 22

*Bring your Quimbanda Magic Mirror, the blessed metal crucifix and the black ritual Quimbanda candle back to your temple.*

*Clean the Quimbanda Magic Mirror and the blessed metal crucifix completely using Cachaca Liquor removing any remaining dirt from the cemetery.*

*Set the Quimbanda Magic Mirror on your altar of the Quimbanda Trinity.*

*Set the blessed metal crucifix into the center of the Quimbanda Magic Mirror.*

*Pour fresh water into the Quimbanda Magic Mirror. The water should come to about ½ inch from the rim of the Quimbanda Magic Mirror bowl.*

*Add 7 drops of Holy Water from a Catholic Church into the Quimbanda Magic Mirror.*

*Place the Quimbanda black ritual candle into a candle holder and place it next to the Quimbanda Magic Mirror.*

*Light the Quimbanda Magic Mirror.*

*Allow the Quimbanda black ritual candle to remain burning until finished.*

*After the Quimbanda black ritual candle has finished burning then cover the Quimbanda Magic Mirror completely with a piece of black cotton cloth.*

*The Quimbanda Magic Mirror should always be covered in black cotton cloth and remain on your altar until you get ready to use it.*

## HOW TO PREPARE A SPIRITUAL BATH BEFORE RITUAL

*Prepare an Amaci herbal bath using 21 herbs sacred to the Spirit, Exu.*

*After preparing the Amaci herbal bath, add a few drops of Eau D' Portugal spiritual cologne into the liquid.*

*Take this spiritual bath before each time that you will be using the Quimbanda Magic Mirror.*

## HOW TO PREPARE A BANISHING BATH AFTER RITUAL

*Prepare an Amaci herbal bath using the 21 herbs sacred to the Spirit Exu or the herb Bay Leaf.*

*The Bay leafs can be boiled in water for 30 minutes in a large metal kettle.*

*After boiling the Bay Leafs then allow the liquid mixture to cool before using.*

*Take this spiritual bath after each time that you will be using the Quimbanda Magic Mirror.*

## HOW TO MAKE BRAZILIAN QUIMBANDA AMACI BATH

The number of fresh herbs used in the preparation of the Quimbanda Spirit Amaci depends on the particular Congo spirit being petitioned and or invoked.

The spirit Exu uses 21 sacred herbs to prepare his particular Quimbanda Spirit Amaci.

The following herbs were substituted from the original Grimoire of Chico Ita-Montenegro because Brazilian herbs used in practical magical applications are difficult to find in the United States.

All of the following 21 herbs are sacred to the Spirit Exu:

*ROMPE SARAGUEY, PARAISO, SALVIA, CAJA, SAUCO BLANCO, VENCE BATALLA, ARTEMISA, SALVIA, ESCOBA AMARGA, VENCEDOR, ROMPE SARAGUEY, ROMPE CAMISA, ARTEMISA, LAUREL, ABRE CAMINO, GUAYABA, BOTON DE ORO, PEREJIL, HIERBA BUENA, PRODIJIOSA, ROMERILLO, PARAISO, HIGUERETA*

## ITEMS NECESSARY

1. *ONE LARGE BOWL*
2. *TWENTY-ONE GRAINS OF PARADISE*
3. *BEE'S HONEY*
4. *POWDERED SMOKED FISH*
5. *POWDERED SMOKED POSSUM*
6. *CIGARS*
7. *CACHACA LIQUOR*
8. *(4) PIECES OF COCONUT SHELLS FOR DIVINATION*
9. *ONE STRAW MAT*
10. *PEMBA*
11. *FRESH HERBS*
12. *FRESH WATER*
13. *HOLY WATER*
15. *COCONUT WATER*
16. *HOLY WATER FROM A CHURCH*

### PREPARATION

1. Lay the straw mat on the floor.

2. Place the large bowl which you will be preparing the Quimbanda Spirit Amaci into the center of the straw mat.

3. Pour all of the waters into the bowl.

4. Place all of the herbs on the mat.

5. Spray the herbs with Cachaca Liquor and blow the smoke from a cigar over all of the herbs.

6. Place all of the items which you will be using to prepare the Quimbanda Spirit Amaci on the mat.

7. Light a white candle and place it next to the bowl.

8. Pick up all of the herbs in both of your hands and hold them up to the sky and say and do the following:

*AGO - WITH THE BLESSINGS OF NZAMBI - SARAVA*

*AGO - WITH THE BLESSINGS OF THE EGUN SPIRITS (DECEASED FAMILYMEMBERS) WHO ARE KNEELING AT THE FOOT OF NZAMBI - SARAVA*

*AGO - WITH THE BLESSING AND PERMISSION OF THE SPIRIT ALUVAIA - SARAVA*

*AGO - WITH THE BLESSING AND PERMISSION OF THE SPIRIT NKOSI MUKUMBE - SARAVA*

*AGO - WITH THE BLESSING AND PERMISSION OF THE SPIRIT MUTALAMBO - SARAVA*

*AGO - WITH THE BLESSING AND PERMISSION OF THE SPIRIT GONGOBIRA - SARAVA*

*AGO - WITH THE BLESSING AND PERMISSION OF THE SPIRIT KATENDE - SARAVA*

*AGO - WITH THE BLESSING AND PERMISSION OF THE SPIRIT ZAZE - SARAVA*

*AGO - WITH THE BLESSING AND PERMISSION OF THE SPIRIT KAVIUNGO - SARAVA*

*AGO - WITH THE BLESSING AND PERMISSION OF THE SPIRIT ANGORO - SARAVA*

*AGO - WITH THE BLESSING AND PERMISSION OF THE SPIRIT KITEMBO- SARAVA*

*AGO - WITH THE BLESSING AND PERMISSION OF THE SPIRIT MATAMBO - SARAVA*

*AGO - WITH THE BLESSING AND PERMISSION OF THE SPIRIT KISIMBI - SARAVA*

*AGO - WITH THE BLESSING AND PERMISSION OF THE SPIRIT KAITUMBA - SARAVA*

*AGO - WITH THE BLESSING AND PERMISSION OF THE SPIRIT KARUNGA NJAMBI - SARAVA*

*AGO - WITH THE BLESSING AND PERMISSION OF THE SPIRIT ZUMBARANDA - SARAVA*

*AGO - WITH THE BLESSING AND PERMISSION OF THE SPIRIT WUNJE - SARAVA*

*AGO - WITH THE BLESSING AND PERMISSION OF THE SPIRIT LEMBA DILE - SARAVA*

*AGO - WITH THE BLESSING AND PERMISSION OF THE SPIRIT EXU - SARAVA*

9. After saying the above prayer, kiss the herbs in your hands three times and then begin to pull off all of the leaves and place them into the bowl.

10. Sitting in a chair in front of the bowl, begin ripping and tearing the herbs in the waters.

11. Sing the following mambo while making the Quimbanda Spirit Amaci:

*KAMA MA IYA - IYA IYA*
*KAMA MA ENU - ENU ENU*
*KAMA MA EBO - EBO EBO*
*KAMA MA EBO - EBO EBO*
*MA MA MA IYA IYA IYA.*
*MA MA MA IYA IYA IYA.*
*MA MA MA IYA IYA IYA.*
*EBO EBO EBO EBO EBO*
*EBO EBO EBO EBO EBO*
*EWE EWE EWE EWE EWE*
*EWE EWE EWE EWE EWE*
*MA MA MA IYA IYA IYA.*
*MA MA MA IYA IYA IYA.*
*MA MA MA IYA IYA IYA.*
*EBO EBO EBO EBO EBO*
*EBO EBO EBO EBO EBO*
*EWE EWE EWE EWE EWE*
*EWE EWE EWE EWE EWE*

***-REPEAT THIS SONG UNTIL YOU HAVE FINISHED PREPARING THE QUIMBANDA SPIRIT AMACI-***

12. When you have finished, add the following items into the Quimbanda Spirit Amaci liquid; honey, grains of paradise, smoked fish and possum.

13. Check with the four coconut shell pieces in the divination ritual to see if the Quimbanda Spirit Amaci has been prepared correctly.

14. If the answer comes with a "yes" then drip into the Quimbanda Spirit Amaci, 21 drops of candle wax into the Amaci liquid.

**-THE CANDLE WAX SEALS THE MAGICAL POWER (AXE) OF HERBS INTO THE SACRED *QUIMBANDA SPIRIT AMACI*-**

*TO DETERMINE IF THE QUIMBANDA SPIRIT AMACI WAS PREPARED CORRECTLY AND ACCEPTED BY THE QUIMBANDA SPIRITS BY USING THE FOUR PIECES OF COCONUT SHELLS DO THE FOLLOWING DIVINATION RITUAL.*

## SACRED DIVINATIONS OF QUIMBANDA

In the Quimbanda religious tradition, divination is used by religious practitioners as a form of communication between the world of the living and the dead. Divination is the attempt to gain insight into a question or situation by way of a standardized process or ritual. It is an integral part of the Quimbanda religious tradition. If a distinction is to be made between divinations and fortune-telling, divination has a formal or ritual and often social character, usually in a religious context, as seen in traditional African medicine; while fortune-telling is a more everyday practice for personal purposes. Particular divination methods vary by culture and religion.

Divination by cowrie seashells has been used for thousands of years by African Priests to determine the spiritual ailment and destiny of an individual. In the Quimbanda religious tradition, the initiated practitioners use several different distinct types of religious divinations. The first form of divination is by use of a set of 16 cowrie shells. The shells are believed to be the mouth piece of the Quimbanda deities and spirits which when interpreted will reveal the past, present and the future destiny of an individual. The divination of the seashells is known to Congo religion practitioners as "*Vititi Nkobo*". In the Quimbanda religious tradition, seashell divination is also known as the "Chamalongo". The word Chamalongo means "cemetery." The literal translation of the Chamalongo is the divining by means of the spirits from the cemetery and of the spirit nganga. The second form of divination is by the use of four round coconut shells. This form of Quimbanda divination is called "*Vititi Nkandian*". It is also referred to as reading the Chamalongos, but in a short abbreviated form by the Congo Priest. The interpretation of the "*Vititi Nkandian*" after throwing them after a ritual prayer will depend on how the four pieces of Chamalongo coconut shells land and to how they are positioned.

The first pattern is called ***ALAFIA*** (four painted white sides facing up). When the pattern of *Alafia* falls, it means yes and the direct blessings from Nzambi and the Eggun Spirits from Heaven.

The second pattern is called ***ELLIFE*** (Two painted white sides facing up and two black sides facing up). When *Ellife* falls, it means yes and the Congo Priest does not have to throw them again. The third pattern is called ***ITAWA*** (three painted white sides facing up and one black side facing up). When *Itawa* falls, it must be thrown again to ascertain a better response and answer.

If the Congo Priest throws another *Itawa*, it means yes and is interpreted as a double oddu number (*Melli*). It would be translated as "*Itawa Melli*". When a double oddu appears, it comes with twice the force and the client must listen very carefully to the interpretation of the oracle. If the second throw falls with two or four white sides up it means yes. If it falls with four black sides facing up or three black sides facing up it then means no.

The fourth pattern is called **OCANA SODDE** (three black sides facing up and one painted white side facing up). When *Ocana Sodde* falls, it means no.

The fifth pattern is called ***OYEKUN*** (four black sides facing up). When *Oyekun* falls it means no. Both *Ocana Sodde* and *Oyekun* are extremely negative and the individual being consulted should seek a consultation oracle with the 16 Chamalongo Seashells of the Quimbanda Spirit Exu.

## HOW TO MAKE QUIMBANDA RITUAL INCENSE

## (DEFUMADORES)

Mix all of the following ingredients together and place into jar until ready to use for the cleansing ritual. This particular Quimbanda Ritual Cleansing Incense must be burned on top of hot incense charcoals. When burning incense on hot charcoals they must be burned in a metal pan. Do not burn in a ceramic or plastic dish because it will catch fire.

- *Dragons Blood Powder*
- *Camphor Chunks Powder*
- *Resin Church Incense Powder*
- *Rosemary Herb Powder*
- *Lavender Flower Powder*
- *Clove Herb Powder*
- *Cedar Wood Powder*
- *Bay Leaf Herb Powder*

**THE GRAND QUIMBANDA MAGIC MIRROR RITUAL**

<u>*Items needed for the divination ritual*</u>

1. *Quimbanda Magic Mirror*
2. *Fresh Water*
3. *Blessed Holy Water from a Catholic Church*
3. *One Blessed Metal Crucifix*
4. *One Blessed White Candle from a Catholic Church*
5. *One Tobacco Cigar*
6. *One Bottle of Cachaca Liquor or White Rum*

***-THIS RITUAL IS DONE AT 12 MIDNIGHT-***

## Step - 1

Take the ritual Quimbanda spiritual bath before beginning this magical divination ritual.

The spiritual bath ritual should be taken just before 12 Midnight so that you can start *THE GRAND QUIMBANDA MAGIC MIRROR DIVINATION RITUAL* right at 12 Midnight.

## Ritual Step - 2

The *Quimbanda Magic Mirror* ritual should be done facing the East.

Burn *Quimbanda* ritual incense in the magical ritual area where you will be doing the ceremony.

Draw the spirit signature of the *Quimbanda Cross* that represents the *Quimbanda Trinity* on the floor in front of your Quimbanda altar using pemba (chalk).

Sit the *Quimbanda Magic Mirror* into the center of the *Quimbanda Cross*.

Light a white candle that has been blessed in a church and place it next to the side of the *Quimbanda Magic Mirror.*

Using your mouth, spray the Cachaca liquor into the *Quimbanda Magic Mirror,* three times.

Blow the smoke from the cigar into the *Quimbanda Magic Mirror,* three times.

Pour fresh water into the *Quimbanda Magic Mirror* bowl. The water level should be about an inch from the rim of the bowl.

Add 7 drops of *Blessed Holy Water from a Catholic Church*

**Ritual Step - 3**

Using your right hand, tap the ground directly in front of *Quimbanda Magic Mirror* and say the following:

*Ago Exu - Sarava, Ago Exu - Sarava, Ago Exu - Sarava,*

**Ritual Step - 4**

Bless yourself with the blessed metal Crucifix by making the sign of the Catholic Cross and recite the following as you are doing it:

*In the name of the Father, the Son and the Holy Spirit.* Amen

**Ritual Step - 5**

After blessing yourself with the blessed metal crucifix, place it into the water and into the center of the bowl of the *Quimbanda Magic Mirror*.

## Ritual Step - 6

Pick the *Quimbanda Magic Mirror* bowl using both of your hands and stand up.

## Ritual Step - 7

Hold the *Quimbanda Magic Mirror* bowl up high over your head and raise your head up and look towards the Heavens and recite the following:

*It was you O Mighty Nzambi who created the Heavens and the Earth.*

*It was you O Mighty Nzambi who created man.*

*It was you O Mighty Nzambi who came to Earth to deliver us from our enemies.*

*It is you O Mighty Nzambi, who gives me victory over my enemies.*

*Our Father, who art in Heaven, hallowed be thy Name; thy Kingdom come; thy will be done on Earth as it is in Heaven.*

*Give us this day our daily bread; and forgive us our trespasses as we forgive those who trespass against us; and lead us not into temptation, but deliver us from evil. For the Kingdom, the power, and the glory are Yours now and forever. Amen.*

*Hail Mary, full of grace. Our Lord is with thee. Blessed art thou among women, and blessed is the fruit of thy womb, Jesus. Holy Mary, Mother of God, pray for us sinners, now and at the hour of our death. Amen.*

Glory be to the Father, And to the Son, And to the Holy Spirit. As it was in the beginning, is now, And ever shall be, World without end. Amen.

## Ritual Step - 8

After saying the above prayers then carefully set the *Quimbanda Magic Mirror* into the center of the spirit signature of the Quimbanda Cross.

## Ritual Step - 9

Facing the East and using your right hand, touch the rim of the *Quimbanda Magic Mirror* with your fingers in the following places, to the *East*, the *West*, from the *South* and to the *North*.

## Ritual Step - 10

Using your right hand, remove the blessed metal crucifix from the water and kiss it three times and then place the blessed metal crucifix next to the blessed white candle.

## Ritual Step - 11

Using your right hand and fingers start to swirl the water in a clockwise rotation while reciting the following ritual prayer;

*AGO - KING EXU REI DAS ENCRUZILHADAS - SARAVA, Ago - Exu Tranca Ruas, Ago - Exu Sete Encruzilhadas, Ago - Exu Das Almas, Ago - Exu Marabo, Ago - Exu Tiriri, Ago - Exu Veludo, Ago - Exu Morcego, Ago - Exu Sete Gargalhadas, Ago - Exu Mirim,*

*AGO - EXU REI DOS 7 CRUZEIROS - SARAVA, Ago - Exu Tranca Tudo, Ago – Exu Kirombo, Ago - Exu Sete Cruzeiros, Ago – Exu Mangueira, Ago - Exu Kaminaloa, Ago - Exu Sete Cruzes, Ago - Exu 7 Portas, Ago - Exu Meia Noite, Ago - Exu Kalunga,*

*AGO - EXU REI DAS MATAS - SARAVA, Ago - Exu Quebra Galho, Ago - Exu Das Sombras, Ago - Exu Das Matas, Ago - Exu Das Campinas, Ago - Exu Da Serra Negra, Ago - Exu Sete Pedras, Ago - Exu Sete Cobras, Ago - Exu Do Cheiro, Ago - Exu Arranca Toco,*

*AGO - EXU REI KALUNGA - SARAVA, Ago - Exu Porteira, Ago - Exu Sete Tumbas, Ago - Exu Sete Catacumbas, Ago - Exu Da Brasa, Ago - Exu Caveira, Ago - Exu Kalunga Pequena, Ago - Exu Corcunda, Ago - Exu Sete Covas, Ago - Exu Capa Preta,*

*AGO EXU REI DAS ALMAS - SARAVA, Ago-Exu Sete Lombas, Ago - Exu Pemba, Ago - Exu Maraba, Ago - Exu Curado, Ago - Exu Nove Luzes, Ago - Exu 7 Montanhas, Ago - Exu Tata Caveira, Ago - Exu Gira Mundo, Ago - Exu 7 Poeiras,*

*AGO - EXU REI DA LIRA - SARAVA, Ago - Exu Dos Infernos, Ago - Exu Dos Cabares, Ago - Exu Sete Liras, Ago - Exu Cigano, Ago - Exu Ze Pelintro, Ago - Exu Pagao, Ago - Exu Da Ganga, Ago – Exu Male, Ago - Exu Chama Dinheiro,*

*AGO - EXU REI DAS SETE PRAIAS - SARAVA, Ago - Exu Dos Rios, Ago – Exu Das Cachoeiras, Ago - Exu Da Pedra Preta, Ago- Exu Marinheiro, Ago - Exu Do Lodo, Ago - Exu Mare, Ago – Exu Bahiano, Ago - Exu Dos Ventos, Ago - Exu Do Coco.*

*Ago - With the blessings of Aluvaiá, Sarava,*

*Ago - With the blessings of Nkosi Mukumbe, Sarava,*

*Ago - With the blessings of Mutalambô, Sarava,*

*Ago - With the blessings of Gongobira, Sarava,*

*Ago - With the blessings of Katendê, Sarava,*

*Ago - With the blessings of Zaze, Sarava,*

*Ago - With the blessings of Kaviungo, Sarava,*

*Ago - With the blessings of Angorô, Sarava,*

*Ago - With the blessings of Kitembo, Sarava,*

*Ago - With the blessings of Matamba, Sarava,*

*Ago - With the blessings of Kisimbi, Sarava,*

*Ago - With the blessings of Kaitumbá, Sarava,*

*Ago - With the blessings of Karunga Njambi, Sarava,*

*Ago - With the blessings of Zumbarandá, Sarava,*

*Ago - With the blessings of Wunje, Sarava,*

*Ago - With the blessings of Lembá Dilê, Sarava*

*IN THE NAME OF NZAMBI, THE GOD OF THE HEAVENS AND THE EARTH - SARAVA*

*IN THE NAME OF EXU MAIORAL - SARAVA*

*IN THE NAME OF EXU REI - SARAVA*

*IN THE NAME OF MARIA PADILLA REINA - SARAVA*

*IN THE NAME OF MY ANCESTORS WHO ARE KNEELING AT THE FOOT OF YOUR CROSS NZAMBI - SARAVA*

*Reveal my enemies above me, reveal my enemies below me, reveal my enemies in front of me, reveal my enemies behind me, reveal my enemies to the right of me, reveal my enemies to the left of me.*

*Exu of the Crossroads - Sarava*

*Exu of the Crossings - Sarava*

*Exu of the Forest - Sarava*

*Exu of the Cemetery - Sarava*

*Exu of the Souls - Sarava*

*Exu of the Lyres - Sarava*

*Exu of the Beach - Sarava*

*Exu by the power of your sacred eye, reveal my past enemies to me.*

*Exu by the power of your sacred eye, reveal my present enemies to me.*

*Exu by the power of your sacred eye, reveal my future enemies to me.*

*Nzambi, when the cock crowed three times, Judas betrayed you and was revealed.*

*Nzambi as Judas betrayed you and was revealed, so shall you reveal my past enemies.*

*Nzambi as Judas betrayed you and was revealed, so shall you reveal my present enemies.*

*Nzambi as Judas betrayed you and was revealed, so shall you reveal my future enemies.*

*Nzambi, Heaven and Earth shall pass away, but your words will never pass away.*

*Ago - Exu Rei - Sarava*

*Ago - Maria Padilla Reina - Sarava*

*Ago - Exu Rei Kalunga - Sarava*

*Ago - Pomba Gira Reina Kalunga - Sarava*

*Ago - Exu Porteira - Sarava*

*Ago - Exu Sete Tumbas - Sarava*

*Ago - Exu Sete Catacumbas - Sarava*

*Ago - Exu Da Brasa - Sarava*

*Ago - Exu Caveira - Sarava*

*Ago - Exu Kalunga - Sarava*

*Ago - Exu Corcunda - Sarava*

*Ago - Exu Sete Covas - Sarava*

*Ago - Exu Capa Preta - Sarava*

*Ago Exu - Sarava*

*Ago Exu - Sarava*

*Ago Exu - Sarava*

## Ritual Step - 12

When finished reciting the invocation ritual prayers, remove your hand from the water and allow the water to start to settle.

Using the light from the candle, hold it next to the *Quimbanda Magic Mirror* and begin to interpret what you can see.

To move to the next vision in the *Quimbanda Magic Mirror*, just swirl the water around in an up and down motion and start to interpret the sacred oracle as the waters begin to calm.

Do this each and every time that you wish to see more visions in the water of the *Quimbanda Magic Mirror*.

## CONCLUSION OF THE DIVINATION RITUAL

### Ritual Step - 13

Using your right hand, pick up the blessed metal crucifix and kiss it three times.

Place the metal crucifix back into the water and into the center of the *Quimbanda Magic Mirror.*

As you are placing the metal crucifix back into the *Quimbanda Magic Mirror,* recite the following;

*Nzambi, Heaven and Earth shall pass away but your word will never end. Sarava*

### Ritual Step - 14

Cover the *Quimbanda Magic Mirror* using a black cloth and place it on the altar, next to your spirit mysteries until ready to use it again.

The water needs to be replaced and changed in *the Quimbanda Magic Mirror* every seven days.

There should always be a lit blessed white candle burning next to it at all times to give light to the spirits which reside inside the *Quimbanda Magic Mirror*.

## Ritual Step - 15

Take the ritual Quimbanda banishing spiritual bath at the conclusion of *THE GRAND QUIMBANDA MAGIC MIRROR DIVINATION RITUAL.*

*A DIAGRAM OF THE SACRED SPIRIT SIGNATURE OF THE MONTENEGRO MAGIC MIRROR.*

***PAPA MONTENEGRO'S OCCULT SHOP*** would like to invite you to browse through our store and shop with confidence.

Authentic Handmade Occult Products, Quimbanda Ritual Products, Herbal Baths, Colognes, Incense, Oils, Spell Kits, Candles, Books & Sacred Art. All of our occult products are handmade.

*WE CARRY OVER 1800 AUTHENTIC HANDMADE & RITUALLY PREPARED OCCULT OILS IN STOCK AT OUR STORE, MADE WITH REAL MAGICAL HERBS, ESSENTIAL OILS, FRAGRANCED OILS & RARE OCCULT SACRED INGREDIENTS.*

**WWW.PAPAMONTENEGRO.COM**

www.ingramcontent.com/pod-product-compliance
Ingram Content Group UK Ltd.
Pitfield, Milton Keynes, MK11 3LW, UK
UKHW041925190726
13854UKWH00003B/1451

9 781105 803406